Our
Elections

I KNOW AMERICA

Richard Steins

THE MILLBROOK PRESS
Brookfield, Connecticut

Published by The Millbrook Press
2 Old New Milford Road
Brookfield, CT 06804
© 1994 Blackbirch Graphics, Inc.

10 9 8 7 6 5 4

Created and produced in association with Blackbirch Graphics.
Series Editor: Tanya Lee Stone

Library of Congress Cataloging-in-Publication Data
Steins, Richard.
    Our elections / Richard Steins.
       p.   cm. — (I know America)
    Includes bibliographical references and index.
    Summary: Describes the democratic process, the presidential election, and
elections that shaped our country's history.
       ISBN 1-56294-446-0 (lib.bdg.)   ISBN 07613-0092-9(pbk.)
    1. Elections—United States—Juvenile literature. 2. Political parties—United
States—Juvenile literature. [1. Elections. 2. Politics, Practical. 3. United States—
Politics and government.] I. Title. II. Series.
JK1978.S84   1994
324.6'0973—dc20   94-8537
                                                                    CIP
                                                                    AC

Acknowledgments and Photo Credits
Cover: ©Joe Traver/Gamma Liaison; pp. 5, 14, 16, 18, 19, 33: Wide World
Photos, Inc.; p. 7: ©Mark Downey/Liaison International; pp. 9, 12, 22, 25,
37: Collections of the Library of Congress; pp.10, 21: ©Brad Markel/
Gamma Liaison; pp.13, 24: National Portrait Gallery; pp.17, 26, 40:
©Blackbirch Press, Inc.; pp. 20, 28: The Bettmann Archive; p. 30: ©Jon
Levy/Gamma Liaison Network; p. 38: ©Gamma Liaison; p. 44: AP/Wide
World Photos.

CONTENTS

A crowd of a few hundred people stamped their feet to keep warm in the frosty air. It was 2 A.M. on Election Day, Tuesday, November 3, 1992, at an airport in Denver, Colorado. When the plane touched down, the crowd began to cheer wildly. They were waiting for Governor Bill Clinton of Arkansas, the Democratic party's candidate for president of the United States.

Governor Clinton was heading home to Little Rock, where he and his wife, Hillary, would cast their votes in the presidential election as citizens of Arkansas. But before returning to Little Rock, Bill Clinton made this one last stop. He came out of his plane and started to shake hands enthusiastically. After a brief talk, he reboarded his plane for Arkansas.

People all over the United States had gathered at a variety of political rallies throughout 1992 to cheer for their candidates. They had taken part in the most important event in a democratic society—the election of the country's leaders.

What is an election? It is the process by which free citizens select the thousands of men and women they want to run their government—at all levels.

In a democracy, government officials are chosen by the people, and serve for a specific time (a term of office). Depending on state laws, an official may run for re-election once the term is over. But if the voters are displeased, they may vote for someone else, and the official will have to leave office.

Our system of government is also called a representative democracy. American citizens do not directly make governmental decisions; they elect officials to govern for them.

In order to make such choices, citizens need to learn how the candidates feel about the issues of the day. Important issues are discussed on television, newspapers and magazines report on the candidates, and everything they say is analyzed by political writers for the benefit of the voters. Candidates also appear on radio and TV talk shows, where listeners can sometimes call in and ask questions.

On Election Day, your vote is secret. Once you've voted, you await the outcome. Later in the evening, television and radio news shows begin to report on the election, and eventually reporters announce the winners. Your vote has helped choose the people who will lead your city, state, and country.

President-elect Bill Clinton salutes well-wishers in Charlottesville, Virginia, in January 1993.

A DEMOCRATIC PROCESS

The president of the United States is elected every four years. But elections are also held in other years. Most elections in our country are held on the first Tuesday after the first Monday in November. But elections for public offices may be held at any time, depending on state law. The day the election is held in November is popularly called Election Day, even though a city or state may have additional "election days."

Who Gets Elected?

First-time voters are likely to be surprised by the number of people for whom they are asked to vote. Television and radio stations and newspapers devote the most attention to the "big" races. But as a citizen, you will be asked to choose among individuals for many public jobs.

Opposite:
A supporter waves an American flag during a political rally. On Election Day, citizens of the United States vote for their favorite candidates.

7

The following is a partial list of the kinds of positions you may see up for election in your state:

- President of the United States
- Vice president of the United States
- United States senator
- United States representative
- State governor
- Members of the state legislature
- State attorney general
- State comptroller (chief financial officer)
- State judges
- City mayors
- Members of city council
- County or town executives
- County or town district attorney
- County or town judges
- Members of the county or town council
- Sheriff
- Members of the local school board
- Members of other local boards or commissions

On Election Day, not every office on this list will necessarily be on the ballot (list of candidates) for your state. For example, not every state elects judges. In some states, judges are appointed to their positions by the governor. Nor is every office that is on the list up for election at the same time. But at one time or another over the years that you vote, you will be asked to choose women and men to fill offices at many different levels of government.

What Are the Rules for Voting?

The U.S. Constitution and the Congress give very broad guidelines for voting rights. The Twenty-sixth Amendment to the Constitution, adopted in 1971, says that anyone over eighteen is allowed to vote.

In 1965, Congress passed the Voting Rights Act. This law guaranteed that the federal government would step in if any state attempted to deny a citizen's voting rights because of race. As a result of this act, millions of African Americans in the South were allowed to register to vote for the first time.

In 1993, Congress passed the "motor-voter" bill. This law requires states to allow citizens to register to vote (get their names on the list of eligible voters) at

CELEBRATION AT BALTIMORE ON MAY 19ᵗʰ 1870.

This illustration celebrates the passing of the Fifteenth Amendment in 1870, which secured the right to vote for African Americans.

the same time that they apply for a driver's license. States may still allow a few other ways to register (for example, by postcard, or in post offices and banks). But the "motor-voter" law guarantees one method of registration common to all states.

Federal laws about voting try to prevent the states from denying anyone the right to vote. All other laws on voting are left up to the individual states. States, for example, determine the following:

• Dates of elections: States may set dates for elections at times of the year other than November.

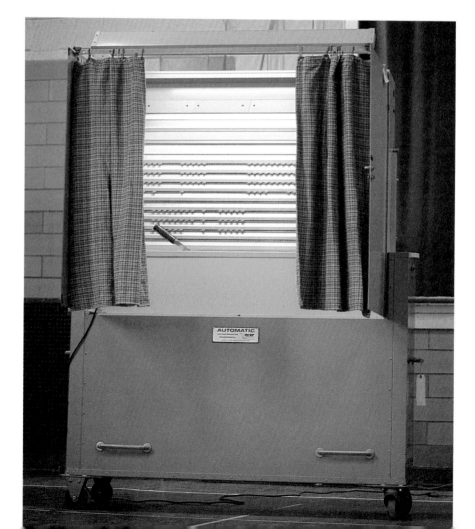

A voting booth stands open in a school gymnasium. Schools are often closed on Election Day so that they can be used as polling places.

- Special elections: States determine if a special election needs to be held. Special elections are held if someone resigns or dies while in office.

- Election rules: States determine election rules. For example, they determine how the winners will be decided and exactly how many votes a candidate must receive in order to be declared the winner.

- Place of the election: States determine where voting takes place. People often vote in schools, general stores, places of business, or lobbies of apartment buildings. States also decide if you vote on a voting machine or by paper ballot. Most voting today is by machine.

- Absentee ballots: State laws also provide for absentee ballots. Absentee ballots are usually paper ballots that are given to any citizen who is going to be out of the state on Election Day but still wants to vote. In order to vote while away, the voter must request an absentee ballot before Election Day. The voter marks the ballot and mails it to the board of elections and it is counted on Election Day.

- Who gets to vote: One of the most important things decided by state law is who gets to vote. The states decide residency requirements, which are rules about how long you need to live in the town, county, or state before you are allowed to vote. They also decide who is not allowed to vote. All states deny the right to vote to anyone who is in prison and to noncitizens of the United States and temporary visitors.

WOMEN AND VOTING

American women were not allowed to vote at the national level until 1920. The Nineteenth Amendment to the Constitution was passed that year, and the following November millions of American women voted in the presidential election for the first time.

During colonial times, some women who owned property did have the right to vote in local elections. But in general, colonial women were not allowed to vote. When the Constitution was written in 1787, it was for the most part left to the states to say who could vote in elections. They, in turn, did not at first give the right to vote to both women and African Americans. A woman's place, many believed, was in the home—not in politics or government.

Suffragettes campaign in 1912.

But women fought for the right to vote from the very beginning of the country's history. Abigail Adams, the wife of President John Adams, urged her husband not to forget the rights of women. On July 19 and 20, 1848, a group of women met in Seneca Falls, New York. They issued a declaration of the rights of women that included a demand for the vote. The leading supporters of this early movement were Elizabeth Cady Stanton and Lucretia Mott.

The women's movement also supported an end to slavery and the prohibition of alcohol. In 1870, five years after the end of the Civil War, the Fifteenth Amendment was passed. This amendment guaranteed the right to vote to African Americans.

In 1869, a new women's group called the National Woman Suffrage Association was formed. (The word *suffrage* means the right to vote.) Its leaders were Susan B. Anthony and Elizabeth Cady Stanton. Some women's leaders wanted an amendment to the

Lucretia Mott

Constitution granting women the vote. Others believed in working at the state level to achieve their goal.

By the early 1900s, women's groups had won the right to vote in twelve states. But there was still no national right to vote. As women began to win the right to vote at the state level, Congress passed a resolution that eventually became the Nineteenth Amendment to the Constitution in 1920.

CAMPAIGNS AND ELECTIONS

An election involves much more than casting a ballot (registering a vote). Election Day is the end of a very long process. Before Election Day, political parties do a great deal of work, including choosing their candidates. Once the candidates are elected, the campaign begins. A campaign is the period before an election when the candidates compete for the attention of the voters.

What Is a Primary?

A primary is an election that chooses a political party's candidate for office. In order to vote in a party's primary, you must be registered as a member of that party (a group of people organized for the purpose of

Opposite: Geraldine Ferraro campaigns for a U.S. Senate seat in New York in September 1992. In 1984, Ferraro was the first woman to run for vice president.

directing the policies of the government). The winner of a primary then goes on to run against other candidates in the final election.

There are many different kinds of primaries, and they are held at all times of the year. For example, at the presidential level, candidates for the presidency in both the Democratic and Republican parties must compete in many state primaries.

Voters in state presidential primaries do not vote directly for the candidate. Instead, they choose a group of delegates (official representatives) who are pledged to vote for a particular candidate at the party's national convention during the summer.

Primaries are also held for other offices. For example, candidates for governor and mayor must often enter primaries. Primaries, however, are a relatively new way of choosing candidates, at least for the office of president. Even as recently as twenty years ago, candidates for office were frequently chosen by a few party officials. Voters had little or nothing to say except on Election Day itself. For example, the 1968 Democratic candidate for president, Hubert H. Humphrey,

Democratic presidential candidate Bill Clinton talks to supporters in Mount Vernon, New York, before that state's primary in March 1992.

won all of his delegates as the choice of state party leaders. He did not run in any state primaries. After he lost the election to Richard M. Nixon, the Democratic party changed its rules. It ordered state Democratic parties to hold primaries for presidential candidates. This change reduced the power of party leaders to choose the presidential candidate.

Caucuses

A caucus is a different way of choosing candidates. Caucuses to choose presidential delegates are held every four years in Iowa and Maine and in a number of other states. In a caucus, voters gather at different places throughout the state. They then divide into groups that support individual candidates. The group supporting one candidate goes to one side of a room, while groups supporting other candidates go to other parts of the same room. The candidate who has the most number of supporters wins the most number of delegates. Unlike votes in primaries, which are secret, a vote in a caucus is made in public.

What Is a Campaign?

A campaign for public office is a time of intense activity before an election, when the candidates present their positions and seek voter support. Candidates appeal to voters in many different ways.

One way is through television. Television ads present the candidate's positions on issues and try to show that he or she is the best choice.

Richard M. Nixon was elected president in 1968 and resigned in 1974.

Candidates often appear on radio and television interview shows in addition to political commercials. Also, the candidates will sometimes debate each other on television or radio.

Candidates still campaign the old-fashioned way as well. The live campaign rally—held before an auditorium full of supporters or even on a street corner—is a time-honored tradition in American politics. Another tradition is the political debate.

On the campaign trail, Secret Service agents watch as Bill Clinton reaches out to a Columbus, Ohio, crowd in July 1992. The Secret Service protects major presidential and vice presidential candidates during their campaigns.

Who Pays for Campaigns?

Political campaigns cost a lot of money. In the past, they were paid for by contributions from a candidate's political supporters. But many people felt that such contributions led to unfair politics. For example, a wealthy individual or private company could give millions of dollars to a campaign. The candidate may then feel as if he or she is obliged to agree with the contributor's views. In order to prevent this from happening in presidential campaigns, Congress passed a number of laws. The government agreed to help pay for a campaign if the individual would accept certain rules. The first was that no person or company could contribute more than $5,000 to a campaign. In return, the government would give the campaign "matching funds" up to a certain amount of money. Even if a candidate raised $10 million, the government would give another $10 million—again as long as no single private gift was more than $5,000.

In the presidential election of 1992, all the candidates except one—Ross Perot, a billionaire who chose to spend his own money on his campaign—accepted the limitations on campaign contributions so they could qualify for matching funds.

Some states also have laws that limit contributions given to campaigns. But the American people want campaigns to cost less and to be more fair. More reform is likely to come in the years ahead.

What Happens on Election Day?

On Election Day, Americans exercise their most treasured right and privilege as citizens in a democratic country. Banks, post offices, and schools might be closed, all depending on the particular laws in your state. Your local board of elections will have sent you a notice telling you the location of your polling place—that is, where you will vote. How long your polling place stays open is a matter of state law. Some states, like New York, keep polling places open from 6 A.M. until 9 P.M.

In an untraditional campaign approach, Ross Perot paid for expensive prime-time, thirty-minute TV commercials in order to deliver his message to voters.

VOTING MACHINES

The first voting machine was used in an election in Lockport, New York, in 1892. But the first machine that recorded votes was invented in 1868 by one of America's greatest inventors, Thomas Alva Edison.

Edison tried to sell his machine to the U.S. Congress. But the lawmakers rejected it for the very reason Edison had invented it—it was too fast! One congressman told Edison that he *wanted* the slow, old-fashioned method of voting because it gave him and his colleagues time to make deals.

Today, most state legislatures have electronic voting machines that are not very different from Edison's design. On each legislator's desk there is a button. His or her

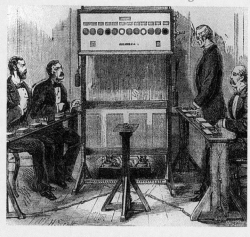

One of the first electronic voting machines.

name is also on a huge board at the front of the room. When the legislator is asked to vote, he or she presses the button and lights go on next to the names on the board. If a red light goes on, the legislator has voted no. A green light means yes. There is also a light to show that a legislator has abstained—that is, chosen not to vote.

The different voting machines for regular elections all work on the same principle. When the voter goes into the voting booth, he or she pulls a master lever or switch that closes the curtain and unlocks the machine. The voter sees a list of the positions and names up for election. The voter pulls the lever next to the name of the candidate he or she chooses for each office. These votes are not recorded in the machine until the master lever is pulled back into its original position, opening the curtain. Many voting machines now use computers to record and count the votes.

The United States was the first country to use voting machines. Although most countries of the world still rely on paper ballots, the voting machine is becoming more common.

Some voters may have to drive miles in order to cast a ballot. Others may simply vote in the lobby of their apartment house. The polling place is run by trained workers paid by the local board of elections. In addition, each party has many unpaid volunteer "watchers" or "challengers" to see that no one votes who isn't supposed to (for example, someone who no longer lives in the town). When you register to vote, your name is placed on an alphabetical list, and each time you vote your name is checked off in the book that lists the voters in your district.

Although some rural areas still use paper ballots, most voting in the United States is done on voting machines. Voting machines vary, but the basic concept remains the same in each model: The name of the candidate appears next to or under a lever or handle. To vote for your candidate, you pull the lever next to his or her name. Your vote is then recorded in the machine.

When the polling hours are over, workers from the board of elections unlock the voting machines. They then record the totals for each candidate and report the results. Depending on state law, absentee ballots—which were mailed before Election Day—are also counted at the central board of elections.

By this time, you may have gone home, finished your dinner, and may be eagerly awaiting news of the election. You hope that your candidate wins. But whatever happens, your single vote will have made a difference in the election process.

A volunteer checks off voters' names from the register.

21

CHAPTER

★ 3

OUR TWO-PARTY SYSTEM

The people who founded the United States believed that political parties were bad for the country. They felt that parties would divide people against each other and harm democracy. No political parties officially existed when the U.S. Constitution was written in the late 1780s. But that soon changed. Within just ten years, the United States had two major political parties.

As the country grew, it became clear that not everyone believed in the same things. We could all be good Americans, but farmers in the South could have different ideas about what was best for the country, while merchants in the North could have others. Although many political parties have come and gone over two hundred years, the United States basically still has a two-party system.

Why Did Political Parties Develop?

In a democratic society, everyone does not agree or have the same point of view about each issue. In early America, for example, many of the country's Founding Fathers wanted a strong central government. They took the side of the merchants, bankers, and business people. Other leaders, however, favored a weaker central government and strong state governments. They sided with the country's many small farmers.

The leading voice for a strong central government was Alexander Hamilton. Hamilton was secretary of the treasury under President George Washington. He and his followers were known as the Federalists. Thomas Jefferson supported small farmers and strong state governments. Jefferson had written the Declaration of Independence and was elected the third president of the United States in 1800. He and his followers were called the Democratic-Republicans. They were also sometimes called Anti-Federalists.

By the time Jefferson was elected, two major political parties existed in the United States. But Jefferson was a better politician than any of the Federalists. He established the Democratic-Republicans as the strongest party. By the time Jefferson left the presidency in 1809, the Federalists were a weak party. The Democratic-Republicans

Alexander Hamilton was the leader of the Federalist party. He and his followers believed in a strong national government.

remained the leading party for almost forty years. By the 1820s, they were known simply as the Democrats, or the Democratic party.

In 1828, the Democratic party candidate, Andrew Jackson, was elected president. Jackson was a strong leader who made many enemies in his eight years in the White House. In 1834, his opponents adopted the name *Whigs*. The Whigs opposed the idea of a powerful presidency. Instead, they wanted Congress to be the strongest branch of government. Beyond that, the Whigs tended not to have strong positions on the issues.

In the election of 1840, the Whig candidate for president, William Henry Harrison, was elected. But Harrison died after only thirty days in office. The Whigs then lost the presidential election of 1844. They won the election of 1848, but their candidate, Zachary Taylor, died in office after little more than a year.

The Whigs were not strong enough to oppose the Democrats. They had been created because of

This illustration shows the log cabin that became the symbol of Harrison's candidacy. William Henry Harrison was called the "log-cabin candidate" because he was content with the simple things in life, unlike his opponent, Martin Van Buren.

Abraham Lincoln was elected president twice under the banner of the Republican party.

their opposition to Jackson. Eventually, they split apart, mainly over the issue of slavery. Proslavery Whigs went back to the Democrats. Many antislavery Whigs joined another new party, formed in 1854, called the Republicans. The Republican party was created to oppose the expansion of slavery in the western territories of the United States. The first Republican to run for president was John C. Frémont, in 1856. He was defeated by the Democrat, James Buchanan. In the 1859 election, however, the

Republicans won the presidency, and Abraham Lincoln became the first Republican president.

The issue of slavery led to the Civil War (1861–1865). By the end of this conflict, the Republican party was the leading party in the nation. Since the years leading up to the Civil War, the Democrats and the Republicans have been the two major parties in the United States.

Who Are the Democrats?
Who Are the Republicans?

Many people today think of the Democrats as the party of average, working-class people and minorities. Many wealthy people, however, are also Democrats. What does the party stand for? On the whole, the Democratic party today stands for a strong federal government and for government programs to help the poor and minorities.

The Republican party, in contrast, is often thought of as the party of the wealthy and of business. Many middle class and poor people, however, consider themselves Republicans. What do Republicans stand for? On the whole, the Republican party believes that the least government is the best government. Its members think that government should interfere as little as possible in people's lives—and especially in the economy.

It may sometimes be difficult to figure out who's a Republican and who's a Democrat. For example, some Democrats are opposed to increasing spending

A 1912 political cartoon called "The Challenge" shows the Bull Moose chasing the Democratic and Republican mascots into the hills.

Since 1800, America has mainly had a two-party system. But there have been attempts to form other political parties. These parties are sometimes called third parties.

No third parties have lasted very long. Almost all were formed around one leading issue and they were supported only by people who felt strongly about that issue. Once an issue was addressed by one or both of the leading parties, a third party would usually disappear.

Third parties play an important role in our democracy. By highlighting an issue that may have been ignored, they help educate the country and force the leading parties to take action.

One of the most colorful third-party challenges came from a former president. In 1912, the Republican National Convention nominated President William Howard Taft for a second term. Republicans who believed Taft was too conservative formed the Progressive party and nominated former president Theodore Roosevelt as their candidate. When Roosevelt said he was as strong as a bull moose, the party was unofficially called the Bull Moose party.

In the election, the Bull Moose party came in second, ahead of the Republicans. Because the Republicans were so bitterly divided, the Democrats, under Woodrow Wilson, won. As president, Wilson enacted much of the program of the Bull Moose party. As a result, the party never again enjoyed the success it had in 1912.

One important third-party movement occurred in the 1992 election. Ross Perot decided to challenge the Democrats and Republicans. He claimed that government had become ineffective under the two major parties. Perot captured 19 million popular votes.

on government programs, while some Republicans support these programs. Why does this confusion exist?

The reason is that our two major political parties are like enormous tents that are able to hold a large number of people who have different points of view. In order to be a Republican or a Democrat, you don't necessarily have to agree with all of the principles that the majority of people in your party support. People within a political party are allowed to disagree with each other.

How Do I Join a Party?

When you turn eighteen you may register to vote. When you register, you will be asked to declare which political party you belong to. By doing so, you "join" the party. You are asked to join a party because many states require that information before you are allowed to vote in a party's primary. If you declare that you are a Democrat, then you will be allowed to vote in Democratic primaries that select the party's nominees. If you say you are a Republican, you can vote in Republican primaries.

If you do not wish to be a member of any party, you may say you are an "independent." However, in most states you will then not be permitted to vote in primaries. More recently, however, a number of states have adopted "open primaries." An open primary is one in which all voters, regardless of party, are allowed to vote.

ELECTING OUR PRESIDENT

We have already seen how candidates for the office of president of the United States compete for convention delegates in primaries. This exhausting period before a party's national convention is only the first part of the campaign season. In November, the nominees must face each other in the final election. The winner becomes our president for the next four years.

What Happens at a National Convention?

Because of the modern primary system, a party's nominee is almost always known before a national convention meets. At today's conventions, the nominee is always chosen on the first ballot. He or

Opposite:
During the last day of their national convention in July 1992, Democrats celebrate the official nomination of Bill Clinton as their candidate for president.

she has arrived at the convention with a majority of delegates elected in state primaries and caucuses. It is possible for a candidate *not* to have a majority of delegates by the time a convention meets. But no Democratic or Republican candidate since 1952 has required more than one ballot to be nominated.

In the days when party leaders chose presidential candidates, the nominee would often not be known until the convention voted. In 1924, for example, the Democratic National Convention took 124 ballots—and two weeks—to nominate John Davis as its candidate for president. The party was deeply divided, and none of the leading candidates could get enough votes to win nomination. Davis, a relatively unknown lawyer, was chosen as a compromise candidate. But he went on to lose the November election overwhelmingly to Calvin Coolidge.

The convention also must nominate the vice presidential candidate. But even this event lacks suspense, since the vice presidential candidate is always selected by the presidential nominee. The convention delegates merely ratify (approve) the choice.

Delegates to the convention also hear dozens of speeches by party leaders. The final speech is given by the presidential candidate on the last night of the convention. The final night of the convention is like a big party. When the nominees for president and vice president appear on the stage to address the delegates, thousands of colored balloons fall from the ceiling.

The delegates toot horns, wave banners, and cheer at the top of their lungs for the two people they have nominated for election in November.

Now the candidates begin the most exhausting part of the campaign. They must spend twenty-hour days flying from state to state, addressing supporters and potential voters. They must also attend fund-raising lunches and dinners and ride in motorcades. They have endless press conferences and appear on television and radio interview shows.

What Is the Electoral College?

It may seem odd, but the president and vice president of the United States are *not* really elected on Election Day. They are actually elected by a few hundred people the following December.

In 1960, at the Democratic National Convention, Lyndon B. Johnson celebrates his nomination as vice president. John F. Kennedy, the presidential candidate, is shown in the background (seated right).

WHAT HAPPENS IF NOBODY WINS?

Is it possible that a presidential election could be held and no one would win? Yes. Remember, in our system of government, the president is not elected by the popular vote, but by the Electoral College. If no one wins a majority of the electoral votes, then no one has been elected.

The framers of the Constitution realized that such a possibility existed. In the event that no one gets a majority in the Electoral College, the Constitution states that the president is chosen by the U.S. House of Representatives. In such a case, each state has one vote—and only one vote.

Two elections in our history have been decided by the House of Representatives. The first was the election of 1800, in which the Democratic-Republican party nominated Thomas Jefferson for president and Aaron Burr for vice president. However, 73 electoral votes were won by both of them, making Burr eligible to be president, and leaving the decision to the House of Representatives. At that time, the electors did not vote separately for vice president. The person who received the most electoral votes became president, and the runner-up became vice president. The House of Representatives chose Jefferson as president and Burr as vice president.

In 1804, the Twelfth Amendment to the Constitution was adopted. This amendment ordered the electors to vote for president and vice president separately to prevent a tie within a party.

The second presidential election that was decided by the House of Representatives occurred in 1824. In that election, Andrew Jackson received 42 percent of the popular vote and 99 electoral votes. John Quincy Adams received 32 percent of the popular vote and 84 electoral votes. Two other candidates, Henry Clay and William H. Crawford, split the remaining 78 electoral votes. No one had a majority.

In the House, Clay's supporters voted for Adams. That meant that even though Jackson had come in first, Adams became president.

When you vote for a mayor, senator, or judge, you are voting directly for that person. When you vote for president, however, you are not actually casting a ballot for your candidate. The name does appear in the voting machine, but when you pull the handle next to a presidential candidate's name, you have actually voted for an elector. An elector is a person pledged to vote for your candidate.

This system of electing presidents was established by the U.S. Constitution in 1789. In Article 2, Section 1, the Constitution states: "Each State shall appoint...a Number of Electors, equal to whole Number of Senators and Representatives to which the State may be entitled in the Congress." The electors chosen by each state are called the Electoral College. They are not a college in the usual sense. They are a group of people who officially elect the president and vice president of the United States.

For example, California has fifty-two members in the U.S. House of Representatives and two members in the U.S. Senate. In the Electoral College, therefore, California has fifty-four votes (52 + 2 = 54).

The larger the state, the more votes it has in the Electoral College. Because no state has fewer than one representative, and all states have two senators, the smallest state will still have three electoral votes.

To be elected, a candidate must put together enough states in the election to get a majority (more than half of the total) of the Electoral College. If no candidate wins a majority in the Electoral College, the president is then chosen directly by the House of Representatives.

The electors meet in their home states and cast their votes. Congress is then authorized to count the votes. The Electoral College meets officially in December. Its votes are sealed and sent to the U.S. Senate. When the Congress meets in January, the current vice president of the United States unseals the envelope and announces the results to the Senate.

This is the official moment at which the president and vice president are really elected. Of course, you and every other American have known the results for two months before. On that Tuesday evening in November, television reporters announced the results even before all the votes were counted. Computers were even able to predict the winner based on a small sample of actual votes.

Should the Electoral College Be Abolished?

Many citizens feel that the Electoral College is old-fashioned and should be abolished.

Opponents of the Electoral College also point to a danger: It is possible for a candidate to win the most number of popular votes (votes from the people) and still lose in the Electoral College. In fact, this has happened a number of times in U.S. history—the last time in the election of 1888 between President Grover Cleveland and Benjamin Harrison. When the ballots were counted after that election, Cleveland had received 49 percent of the popular vote, Harrison 48

percent, the Prohibitionist party 2 percent, and the Union Labor party 1 percent. Although Cleveland received the most popular votes, Harrison was elected president. Why? Since the states in which Harrison won were larger, their electors made up a majority in the Electoral College.

There are some strong arguments for keeping the Electoral College. Most presidential elections in U.S. history have been close. Sometimes no more than 1 or 2 percentage points separate the candidates. In 1960, for example, only 119,000 votes out of nearly 69,000,000 separated John F. Kennedy from Richard M. Nixon. But in the Electoral College, Kennedy won a clear victory, with 303 votes to Nixon's 219.

Supporters of the Electoral College believe that in such cases the outcome of the election leaves no doubt who won. If an election is so close in the popular vote that its results could be disputed, the winner would be weakened as president. Such a situation could hurt the country in the long run.

Disputes about the Electoral College are likely to continue. For the time being, however, there is little popular support for changing the system. Many people believe that whatever its shortcomings, the Electoral College has given us more than two hundred unbroken years of stable presidential elections.

5

ELECTIONS THAT SHAPED OUR HISTORY

Every election in which a citizen votes—whether for president or for a local school board—is important. Every election can have an effect on your day-to-day life. But throughout more than two hundred years of U.S. history, certain presidential elections have shaped the direction of our lives more than others. This chapter will talk about some of the most important elections in our country's history.

The Election of 1800

This election made Thomas Jefferson the third president of the United States. It was a major election because it marked the end of the Federalist party's power in the White House and the true beginning of the two-party system.

Opposite: Ronald and Nancy Reagan wave to the crowd during the Republican National Convention in 1980. Reagan was the Republican presidential candidate in 1980 and 1984.

Jefferson believed in a federal government that shared more power with the states. They represented a view of America that differed from that of the Federalists, who believed in a strong federal government.

The Election of 1860

The election of 1860 was a significant one because it prompted a major split in the party system of government. This election led to several states withdrawing from the Union, which divided the nation and helped to bring about the Civil War.

By 1860, the issue of slavery had so divided the country that compromise was impossible. In 1854, the Republican party had been founded on the principle of opposing slavery. In 1860, the Republicans nominated Abraham Lincoln for president. No proslavery Southerner would have anything to do with this party. For the first time, a party was based exclusively in one region of the country—in this case, the North.

To complicate matters, the Democrats split over the issue of slavery. A northern group nominated Senator Stephen A. Douglas, while a southern group nominated John C. Breckinridge. A fourth party—the Constitutional Union party—nominated John Bell.

Abraham Lincoln and Hannibal Hamlin won the controversial election of 1860.

The vote was split among four candidates and Lincoln won the election. Although he received only 40 percent of the popular vote, he won a majority in the Electoral College. Lincoln's election most angered people in the South who were proslavery, and within months, eleven states seceded—or withdrew—from the Union. Under the leadership of Jefferson Davis, they set up a new country called the Confederate States of America.

Lincoln refused to accept the withdrawal of these states. As a result, the country went to war for four years, and 600,000 American lives were lost.

The Election of 1920

The Constitution, written in 1787, left it to the states to set the qualifications for voting. At first, there were property requirements. A person had to own a certain amount of property to be able to vote. By the outbreak of the Civil War, however, all adult white males were allowed to vote in most states. African Americans—even free ones in the North—and women could not.

But the defeat of the South in the Civil War in 1865 led to the adoption of the Fifteenth Amendment, which granted the right to vote to African Americans. It would take another hundred years for African Americans to fully exercise the rights they won in 1860. But their rights did exist in the Constitution.

Women, however, were not legally allowed to vote until the passage of the Nineteenth Amendment in 1920. Why did it take women so long to achieve this fundamental democratic right? The answer is not simple, but one reason was that most of the men who controlled politics and government believed that a woman's place was in the home, and that politics was a man's business.

Such attitudes were hard to change. But the entry of the United States into World War I in 1917 provided the final push for women to vote. During that war, thousands of women worked tirelessly in jobs that men had formerly held. Many women also went to Europe and served as nurses.

With the end of the war in 1918, it became impossible any longer to deny the full rights of citizenship to a group that had served their country so courageously. The election of 1920 was a turning point. Finally, the other half of the population was allowed to walk into the voting booth.

The Election of 1932

The Civil War established the Republicans—"the party of Lincoln"—as the most powerful political party in the entire country. In the seventeen presidential elections that were held between 1860 and 1928, Republican candidates won thirteen times, and Democrats won only four.

In 1932, however, the situation was reversed. The Great Depression that began in 1929 and led to an unemployment rate of 33 percent caused a revolution in politics. In the 1932 election, the

HOW CAN I GET INVOLVED?

Even though you may not vote until you are eighteen, you can still get involved in the political process.

One easy way to take action is to write to your local government leaders or representatives in Congress. You may even write to the White House! If you feel strongly about an issue, your leaders will want to hear from you. Reading letters from the people who they represent is one way government officials keep in touch with how people feel about the issues.

If you wish to write to someone in government, go to your library and ask the librarian for a reference book that has the names and addresses of local, state, and federal government officials. In some cases, for example, the address may be simple: "President Bill Clinton, The White House, Washington, D.C. 20500." Your letter may be answered by the official or by a staff member.

You can also get involved by making sure you are informed about political issues—both in Washington and in your own home town. Reading your newspaper and news magazines and watching news programs on television are ways to learn about the issues facing your city, state, and country.

Political campaigns always need volunteers to address envelopes, hand out campaign literature, and sometimes make phone calls on behalf of the candidate. Volunteering is one of the best ways to participate in the political process.

When you are eighteen, you are eligible to cast your first vote. Voting is perhaps the most important way a citizen can influence his or her government. As you get older, you may even consider running for public office. Although relatively few men and women reach the highest public offices in our country, thousands of others do important work by serving on park commissions, school boards, and countless other government bodies. Many great political careers began with election to a local or state position before the person moved up to higher office.

Whatever you do, remember that our political parties are made up of millions of people just like you. Participation by everyone is essential for democracy to survive.

Franklin D. Roosevelt is sworn in as president by Supreme Court Chief Justice Charles Hughes on January 14, 1933.

Democrats under Franklin D. Roosevelt won an overwhelming victory over the Republicans, who were led by President Herbert Hoover. Roosevelt's election was the start of a twenty-year period in which the Democratic party won the White House and controlled Congress. Although the Republicans have won the presidency many times since the late 1960s, the Democrats still continue to dominate Congress, as they did beginning with the election of 1932.

The Election of 1980

The election of 1980 marked another major change in American politics. In that race, the Democratic president, Jimmy Carter, was overwhelmingly defeated for re-election by Ronald Reagan, a Republican. Although Republican presidential candidates had won elections in the 1950s (Dwight D. Eisenhower) and in 1968 and 1972 (Richard M. Nixon), Reagan's victory was a different kind of change. Reagan campaigned on the promise to reduce the power of the federal government in people's lives. That meant lower taxes, less spending by the government on social programs, less regulation, and more money spent on the military. These policies were known as the "Reagan Revolution." Ronald Reagan was so popular among the people that Congress easily passed his programs, even though the Democrats controlled the House of Representatives and were a strong minority in the Senate.

The Future

Most elections have led to peaceful change. Even when one party suffers a major defeat, the change is peaceful. For example, after Franklin Roosevelt crushed the Republican party in 1932, Herbert Hoover congratulated him and stood next to him when FDR became president on March 4, 1933. This is one of the great strengths of American government. We can disagree. We can even disagree strongly. But in the end, the voters decide, and everyone accepts their decision.

Chronology

1787   U.S. Constitution written. Constitution provides for Electoral College to choose president and vice president. Women and African-American slaves ineligible to vote in most states.

1800   Election of Thomas Jefferson as president by House of Representatives after no one wins majority in Electoral College. Beginning of two-party system.

1824   Election of John Quincy Adams as president by House of Representatives.

1828   Election of Andrew Jackson as president provokes party opposition.

1834   Formation of the Whig party in response to Jackson's strong views.

1848   Seneca Falls declaration of women's rights.

1854   Formation of the Republican party in opposition to expansion of slavery.

1860   Election of Abraham Lincoln as first Republican president. Democratic party splits over slavery.

1869   Founding of National Woman Suffrage Association.

1870   Passage of Fifteenth Amendment to Constitution guaranteeing African-American men the right to vote.

1920   Passage of Nineteenth Amendment granting women across the country the right to vote.

1932   Election of Democrat Franklin D. Roosevelt as president. End of Republican domination of White House and Congress.

1992   Election of Democrat Bill Clinton as president. End of twelve years of Republican rule of White House. Third-party challenge of Ross Perot.

1994   End of forty years of control by the Democrats of the House and the Senate.

For Further Reading

Brown, Gene. *The 1992 Election.* Brookfield, CT: The Millbrook Press, 1992.

Fradin, Dennis B. *Voting and Elections.* Chicago: Childrens Press, 1985.

Johnson, Mary Oates. *The President: America's Leader.* Austin, TX: Raintree Steck-Vaughn, 1993.

Samuels, Cynthia K. *It's a Free Country! A Young Person's Guide to Politics and Elections.* New York: Antheneum, 1988.

Scher, Linda. *The Vote: Making Your Voice Heard.* Austin, TX: Raintree Steck-Vaughn, 1993.

Smith, Betsy C. *Women Win the Vote.* Westwood, NJ: Silver Burdett Press, 1989.

Index